greatest
artists

Grandma Moses

Megan Kopp

www.av2books.com

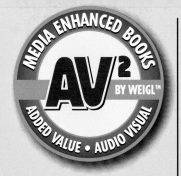

AV² provides enriched content that supplements and complements this book. Weigl's AV² books strive to create inspired learning and engage young minds in a total learning experience.

Your AV² Media Enhanced books come alive with...

Audio
Listen to sections of the book read aloud.

Key Words
Study vocabulary, and complete a matching word activity.

Go to **www.av2books.com**, and enter this book's unique code.

Video
Watch informative video clips.

Quizzes
Test your knowledge.

BOOK CODE

C 2 7 4 2 7 2

Embedded Weblinks
Gain additional information for research.

Slide Show
View images and captions, and prepare a presentation.

AV² by Weigl brings you media enhanced books that support active learning.

Try This!
Complete activities and hands-on experiments.

... and much, much more!

Download the AV² catalog at
www.av2books.com/catalog

AV² Online Navigation on page 32

Published by AV² by Weigl
350 5ᵗʰ Avenue, 59ᵗʰ Floor
New York, NY 10118
Website: www.av2books.com

Library of Congress Cataloging-in-Publication Data
 Names: Kopp, Megan, author.
Title: Grandma Moses / Megan Kopp.
Description: New York : AV2 by Weigl, 2016. | Series: Greatest artists |
   Includes index.
Identifiers: LCCN 2016004406 (print) | LCCN 2016005072 (ebook) | ISBN
   9781489646217 (hard cover : alk. paper) | ISBN 9781489650320 (soft cover :
   alk. paper) | ISBN 9781489646224 (Multi-user ebk.)
Subjects: LCSH: Moses, Grandma, 1860-1961--Juvenile literature. |
   Painters--United States--Biography—Juvenile literature.
Classification: LCC ND237.M78 K67 2016 (print) | LCC ND237.M78 (ebook) | DDC
   759.13--dc23
LC record available at http://lccn.loc.gov/2016004406

Printed in the United States of America in Brainerd, Minnesota
1 2 3 4 5 6 7 8 9 0   20 19 18 17 16

032016
210316

Editor: Heather Kissock   Art Director: Terry Paulhus
Validator: Christina Roman, Galerie St. Etienne

Weigl acknowledges Getty Images, iStock, Newscom, Look and Learn, and Corbis as its primary image suppliers for this title.
Grandma Moses images copyright ©2016 Grandma Moses Properties Co., New York
Page 16: The Metropolitan Museum of Art, Bequest of Mary Stillman Harkness, 1950 (50.145.375)
Page 19: The Phillips Collection, Washington, D.C.
Quotes from Grandma Moses: My Life's History copyright ©1952 (renewed 1980) Grandma Moses Properties Co., New York.

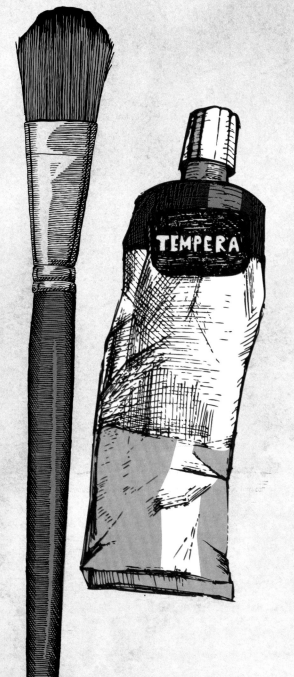

CONTENTS

Meet Grandma Moses

Upon retiring from farm life in her mid-70s, Grandma Moses started embroidering pictures on cloth with woolen thread. When it became too difficult to hold a needle because of her arthritis, she picked up a paintbrush.

Anna Mary Robertson Moses, also known as Grandma Moses, was in her seventies when her career as an artist began. She painted simple scenes stemming from happy childhood memories and from stories she had read or heard. Over the next 20-plus years, this spry artist would take her **folk art** to the masses. Fans of her work included well-known musician Cole Porter and President Harry S. Truman.

Come On Old Topsy

Country life was the focus of most of Grandma Moses' works. Farms, animals, and country folk were common subjects in her paintings.

Grandma Moses was a self-taught artist. She painted "from the top down." She started with the sky and then worked her way down into the details of the painting.

Most of Grandma Moses' paintings are **landscapes**, and all of her pictures tell a story. She liked using bright color, action, and a dash of humor in her portrayals of simple farm life. By the early 1940s, her paintings had evolved into large, **panoramic** portraits of **rural** activities. Her subjects included everything from bringing in the harvest, to tapping sugar maple trees, to sledding and picnicking.

People continue to be drawn to Grandma Moses' paintings of simpler times.

Early Life

Anna Mary Robertson was born on September 7, 1860, in Greenwich, New York. She was the third oldest of Russell King Robertson and Margaret Shannahan's 10 children. Anna Mary's father was a farmer who also ran a flax mill. Her brothers helped out at the mill and on the farm. Anna Mary and her sisters were taught the skills needed to run the home. As the oldest girl, Anna Mary was responsible for helping around the house and looking after the younger children.

Her duties at home meant that Anna Mary could not attend school on a regular basis. She went only when she could be spared from her chores and when the weather was good. Her school was a simple one-room country schoolhouse where all children and all grade levels were taught by one teacher at the same time.

Life was difficult for the Robertson family. With 10 children in the house, **luxuries** were rare, and even necessities were sometimes at a premium. It was often a struggle to make ends meet. The family also experienced its share of tragedy. Two of Anna Mary's brothers and one of her sisters did not live beyond childhood.

The schoolhouse Anna Mary attended is now a museum devoted to her life and art.

Still, Anna Mary's parents worked hard to create a loving home for their children and to provide opportunities for them to learn. Anna Mary's father was an amateur artist. He encouraged all of his children to paint and enjoyed seeing their artwork around the home. Instead of buying them candy, he would buy large pieces of paper for a penny a sheet. The children would use lemon and grape juice as paint. Anna Mary enjoyed creating these artistic projects. She liked to call her art pieces "lambscapes."

"I was happy and contented, I knew nothing better and made the best out of what life offered."

Even though life on the farm was hard work, Anna Mary remembered it as a happy time. She came to love nature, and living and working on the land. When she was 12 years old, Anna Mary left home. Using her cooking, cleaning, and mending skills, she spent the next 15 years working as a live-in housekeeper for wealthy families.

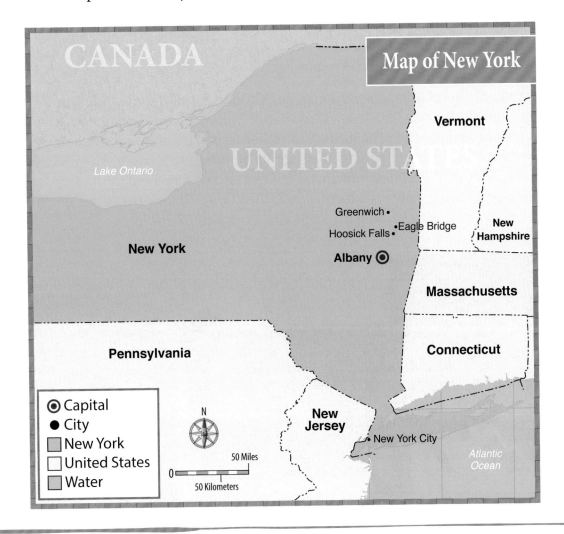

Map of New York

Growing Up

Although Anna Mary's teen years and early twenties revolved around work, she was always making keen observations. One of the families that she worked for noticed her interest in their collection of Currier & Ives **prints**. Produced by the Currier & Ives Company, the pictures depicted the history and customs of early America in a straightforward style. The family gave Anna Mary some art materials, including chalk and wax crayons, to create her own drawings.

Currier & Ives produced more than 1 million prints over its 72-year history. The prints sold for between 5 cents and 3 dollars at the time.

At age 27, Anna Mary met and married Thomas Salmon Moses. He was working on the same farm as a hired hand. The couple moved to Staunton, Virginia, and worked as **tenants** on another farm. Staunton is located in the Shenandoah Valley, a region known for its picturesque scenery. Anna Mary fell in love with the Shenandoah Valley. The couple remained in the area for almost 20 years, eventually buying their own farm. During that time, Anna Mary gave birth to 10 children. Only five lived past infancy.

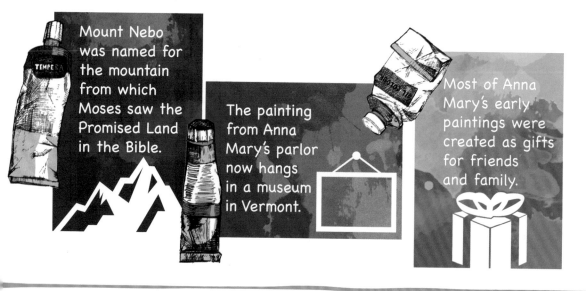

Mount Nebo was named for the mountain from which Moses saw the Promised Land in the Bible.

The painting from Anna Mary's parlor now hangs in a museum in Vermont.

Most of Anna Mary's early paintings were created as gifts for friends and family.

The Mount Nebo farm is still owned by the Moses family. It is the home of Will Moses, Anna Mary's great-grandson, who is also an artist.

Anna Mary kept herself busy with farm work. She made extra money by selling handmade potato chips and fresh butter. Over time, Anna Mary became a popular face in the community. Many of her neighbors began to call her "Mother Moses."

> "I look back on my life like a good day's work. It was done and I am satisfied with it."

Anna Mary would have been content to spend the rest of her life in Virginia. Thomas, however, was homesick. In 1905, he persuaded his wife to return north. They bought a farm in Eagle Bridge, New York, not far from where Anna Mary was born. They named their farm Mount Nebo. Anna Mary used her artistic skills to decorate their home, even painting a picture on the **fireboard** in the parlor.

In 1927, Thomas died suddenly of a heart attack. Now 67 years old, Anna Mary took over running the farm with the help of her youngest son. In 1932, she went for an extended visit with her daughter, who was ill with tuberculosis. Looking to stay busy, Anna Mary began embroidering scenes for friends and family before switching from needle to paintbrush.

Grandma Moses applied her knowledge of embroidery techniques to her paintings. As in embroidery, she used blocks of color and also layered colors side by side to create shades.

Learning the Craft

From the beginning of her painting career, Anna Mary created what is known as primitive art. This meant that it lacked the skill of a trained artist. Her first artworks were small, simple pieces. Some were just copies of existing images. These works usually focused on a single object, such as a bridge or a building.

As her confidence and artistic abilities developed, Anna Mary's paintings reached another level. She began to create art that recalled scenes and activities from her childhood. Her paintings usually showed seasonal, rural activities such as harvesting, chopping wood, and **sugaring**. Other recurring themes included holidays such as Thanksgiving and Christmas.

Grandma Moses would sometimes add glitter to her winter scenes to make the snow sparkle.

Grandma Moses did not include modern conveniences, such as telephone poles, in her paintings.

Until she turned 101, Grandma Moses did her best to spend at least part of every day painting.

When starting a new painting, Anna Mary would begin by cutting a board to fit whatever frame she had chosen. She used Masonite board, which is made from wood fibers formed into hard panels. The **tempered** side was strong and somewhat waterproof, making it a good painting surface. She would treat the board with linseed oil to preserve the wood. Then, she applied three coats of white house paint to the board. Once the house paint dried, she would begin to pencil her idea for the painting onto the white surface.

Anna Mary often painted in her kitchen, with the Masonite laid out flat on the table. Her **palette** was determined largely by the season she was painting. Winter scenes were made up mostly of whites and cool **tones**. Colors could occasionally be seen in people's clothing and various objects in the distant landscape. For paintings of autumn scenes, she used browns. Light green was her color of choice for paintings of spring, while deep green was used to bring summer scenes to life.

Grandma Moses' winter scenes, with their crisp tones, were especially popular. Fans often wrote her to receive copies of her winter-themed paintings, including *Early Snow*.

Early Achievements

*A*nna Mary was a dedicated painter and, before long, had more paintings than room to display them. She gave some of her paintings away, but others were sold for small sums of money. One year, she entered both her paintings and her jams in contests at the county fair. The jams came away with winning ribbons. The art did not.

In 1937, Anna Mary was asked to contribute to a display of art by local women in a drugstore in Hoosick Falls, a nearby village. The following year, a man named Louis Caldor came across Anna Mary's paintings while traveling through Hoosick Falls. At the time, they were priced from $3 to $5. Caldor was an amateur art collector, and he liked what he saw. He bought all of the paintings and then went to the farm to meet Anna Mary. When he told her that he would make her famous, Anna Mary's family thought he was out of his mind.

Caldor was determined, however. He returned to his home in New York and began showing Anna Mary's paintings to local art galleries. He wanted the galleries to **exhibit** and sell her art. The gallery owners declined. They felt it would be a waste of their time and money to plan an exhibit for an artist as old as Anna Mary. They thought Anna Mary's productive years were already behind her.

The town of Hoosick Falls is made up of a village and several smaller outlying communities. Approximately 6,700 people call the area home.

Caldor did not give up. In 1939, three of Anna Mary's paintings were included in an exhibition at the Museum of Modern Art. A solo show of Anna Mary's work, called "What a Farm Wife Painted," was held at Galerie St. Etienne the following year. One month after the show, New York's Gimbels department store featured Anna Mary's work in its Thanksgiving festival. When she came to take part in the festival, Anna Mary promoted not only her art, but her preserves and homemade jam as well. New Yorkers were captivated, and Anna Mary soon had a growing fan base. The press began calling her Grandma Moses.

Like many New York department stores of the time, Gimbels sold art, with its gallery located on the fifth floor.

Master Class

The secret behind Grandma Moses' success was her ability to create homey scenes of country life. People were enchanted with her idyllic scenes of a hardworking, fun-loving American past. Even though her painting lacked the finesse of professionally trained artists, Grandma Moses used specific techniques and strategies to draw her audience into the activities and events taking place in her paintings.

Grandma Moses Goes to the Big City

Unity

Visual unity is the feeling of harmony between all parts of a painting. It occurs when all of the painting's components are working together to bring the picture together. Grandma Moses used clusters of shapes to create unity in her paintings. Often, the same colors were used throughout the painting. This, too, brought unity to the work. Grandma Moses also unified her paintings by exploring specific themes, including holidays and special events.

Repetition

Grandma Moses used repetition in her paintings to create a sense of flow. Repeating elements such as color, shapes, and space creates patterns and helps to produce a visual rhythm. This encourages the viewer's eyes to continue moving across the painting. It can also introduce an element of excitement to the work.

Country Fair

Color

Grandma Moses' use of color is known for its purity. When beginning a new painting, she would start with solid, bright colors. These colors were then modified by adding white to make tints and black to make shades. By doing this, she established a color palette that remained visually interesting while also adding **dimension** to the work. Her use of color and shades also set the mood of the painting.

Apple Butter Making

Space

Space refers to the feeling of depth in a painting. Grandma Moses used several types of perspective to give her paintings a sense of space. When she wanted buildings and other objects to appear far away, she would paint them small in size. This technique is called diminishing perspective. To create a sense of distance, Grandma Moses often painted blue, hazy mountains in the background. This effect is a form of atmospheric perspective. It mimics the effect that atmosphere has on faraway objects.

A Blizzard

Grandma Moses was a **prolific** artist. By the end of her career, she had painted almost 1,600 works. Many of these paintings have become known around the world.

Thanksgiving Turkey

Painted in 1943, *Thanksgiving Turkey* captures the activities surrounding a well-known Thanksgiving tradition. A group has gathered in the yard to catch a turkey for dinner. Children and adults alike attempt to make the catch, while the turkeys try to escape grasping hands. The use of color highlights both the season and the action taking place, with the bright clothing of the people punctuating the cool whites and grays of the scenery.

DATE: 1943 **MEDIUM:** Oil on wood **SIZE:** 15 1/8 x 19 1/8 inches (38.4 x 48.6 centimeters)

Sugaring Off

Sugaring Off is one of Grandma Moses' larger landscapes. Collecting sap from the sugar maples was one of Grandma Moses' favorite subjects, and she created several paintings around this theme. Painted in 1943, this piece highlights men, women, and children all working together in a busy, yet focused, environment.

The painting showcases many of the activities involved in making maple sugar and syrup. Men stand by the trees collecting the buckets of sap. Horse-drawn sleds carry the buckets to the sugar shack so the sap can be boiled and made into syrup. A mother pours maple syrup onto the snow so that it will harden and become candy for the children. As the work goes on, more neighbors arrive to take part in the festivities. The painting captures the sense of community found in rural life.

DATE: 1943 **MEDIUM:** Oil on wood **SIZE:** 23 x 27 inches (58.3 x 68.5 cm)

Moving Day on the Farm

Reflecting on her life as a farm wife and mother to a large family, *Moving Day on the Farm* shows a family helping neighbors move. Activity fills the canvas as people come together to lend a helping hand. The painting demonstrates that, even though moving can be disruptive, it is also full of excitement. Still, while one household is undergoing a change, life goes on for others. This is noted by the farmers harvesting their crops in the background. Grandma Moses completed the work in 1951.

DATE: 1951 **MEDIUM:** Oil on wood **SIZE:** 17 x 22 inches (43.2 x 55.9 cm)

McDonnell Farm

McDonnell Farm was inspired by the popular children's nursery rhyme, "Old MacDonald Had a Farm." Completed in 1943, the work provides insight into life on a farm. Scattered throughout the landscape are farmers in their fields. All are busy at work, whether cutting the grass with a scythe, harvesting the crop, or loading a hay wagon. The role animals play on the farm is also accented, with both horses and cattle used to till fields and haul materials. To the right, a group of children play together, indicating that farm life was not always about work. The colors are muted, but express a sense of unity between the environment and the people in it.

DATE: 1943 **MEDIUM:** Oil on wood **SIZE:** 24 x 30 inches (60.9 x 76.2cm)

Timeline of Grandma Moses

1860

Anna Mary Robertson is born in Greenwich, New York, on September 7 to Russell King Robertson and Margaret Shannahan Robertson. She is the third of ten children and the oldest daughter.

1887

Anna Mary marries farm worker Thomas Salmon Moses on November 9. The couple moves to Staunton, Virginia, shortly after. They remain in the area for almost 20 years before returning to New York in 1905.

1927

Thomas Salmon Moses dies of a heart attack on January 15. Anna Mary continues to run the Mount Nebo farm with the help of her youngest son.

1930s

After arthritis makes embroidering too difficult, Anna Mary begins to paint. She shows her work at local fairs and charity sales.

1938

Louis Caldor sees Anna Mary's paintings in a drugstore window while visiting Hoosick Falls. He purchases all of her paintings and vows to make Anna Mary famous.

1940

The Galerie St. Etienne in New York City stages the first solo showing of Grandma Moses' art. The show is called "What a Farm Wife Painted."

1949

Grandma Moses meets President Harry S. Truman in May, when she travels to Washington, D.C., to receive the Women's National Press Club Award for Outstanding Accomplishment in Art.

1961

Grandma Moses dies on December 13 in Hoosick Falls, New York, at the age of 101.

Path to Success

The Moore Institute of Art, Science and Industry is the country's first and only women's visual arts college. Until 1960, it was housed in Philadelphia's Edwin Forrest Mansion.

Grandma Moses' appearance at Gimbel's New York Thanksgiving festival was a turning point in her career as an artist. Art critics, gallery owners, and the general public all became fascinated with this homespun grandmother and her art. This led to numerous accolades. The year following her New York debut, Grandma Moses won the New York State Prize for her painting, *The Old Oaken Bucket*. In 1944, Galerie St. Etienne devoted two exhibitions to Grandma Moses' art. The gallery also sponsored traveling exhibitions of her work that toured throughout the United States. This eventually led to exhibitions in Europe as well.

In 1946, Otto Kallir, the owner of Galerie St. Etienne, edited a book called *Grandma Moses, American Primitive*. This book provided insight into the paintings of Grandma Moses, along with notes from the artist herself. It quickly became a bestseller. Grandma Moses' autobiography, *My Life's History*, was published in 1952. For those who could not afford to purchase actual paintings, there were prints, posters, collector plates, and even fabrics featuring Grandma Moses' art.

Grandma Moses received honorary **doctoral degrees** from Russell Sage College, in New York, and from the Moore Institute of Art, Science and Industry, in Philadelphia. The National Press Club cited her as one of the five most newsworthy women of 1950. In 1953, she was featured on the cover of *Time Magazine*.

Throughout all the attention, Grandma Moses continued to paint. In 1956, she was **commissioned** to paint a gift for President Dwight D. Eisenhower. In 1961, *The Grandma Moses Storybook* was published. The book contains stories and poems by 28 writers accompanied by reproductions of Grandma Moses' paintings.

The storybook was one of the last projects Grandma Moses would ever work on. Now a centenarian, her health began to fail in the summer of 1961, after taking a fall at her home. She was admitted to hospital and remained there until her death on December 13.

The Creative Process

Artists are creative people. They have vivid imaginations and are able to think in abstract ways. Still, in order to create, they must have a process, or series of steps to follow. While most artists will adapt the process to suit their individual needs, there are basic steps that all artists use to plan and create their works.

Gathering Ideas
Observing and taking inspiration from surroundings

Researching
Studying the subject or topic to determine the approach

Forming Intent
Deciding on a subject or topic to explore

Planning the Work
Obtaining the materials needed to create the work

Outlining the Project
Sketching or developing a model to follow

Creating the Work
Applying the previous stages to the creation of the final product

Making Revisions
Changing elements that are not working

Requesting Feedback
Asking for opinions from others

Completing the Work

Grandma Moses' Legacy

Grandma Moses

6c U.S. Postage

Besides being issued as a postage stamp, *July Fourth* was also chosen to hang in the White House, in Washington, D.C.

Grandma Moses' paintings can be seen in galleries, in museums, and on a variety of products. They have been marketed as print reproductions and greeting cards, and on plates and fabrics. Her paintings continue to appeal to the general public and art collectors alike. As they have gained popularity, their value has also increased. In 2006, a version of *Sugaring Off* was sold for $1.36 million.

Besides being colorful and full of action, Grandma Moses' paintings reflect a simpler time and way of life. They put people in touch with the pioneers that helped to build the United States and the traditions that they honored. By viewing Grandma Moses' works, people learn how Americans lived in the past and what they valued. Through her paintings, Grandma Moses recorded elements of the past for future generations.

See It Now, with host Edward R. Murrow, ran on U.S. television from 1951 to 1958.

Even though Grandma Moses painted scenes from the past, she was open to new technologies created during her lifetime. In fact, she became one of the first artists to reach a mass audience through radio, film, and the then-new medium of television. In 1950, she was the subject of a documentary film, which was later nominated for an Academy Award. A few years later, she appeared as a guest on *See It Now*, a television program hosted by journalist Edward R. Murrow. These appearances helped Grandma Moses to reach a wider audience than artists who had come before her. They also made her art more accessible to the general public.

Grandma Moses has been remembered in a variety of ways. In 1969, the United States Postal Service honored her with a postage stamp that features her painting *July Fourth*. Fellow artist Norman Rockwell immortalized her in his painting *Christmas Homecoming,* which appeared on the cover of *The Saturday Evening Post* in December 1948. Grandma Moses' paintings continue to hang in galleries, museums, and homes around the world.

Grandma Moses became friends with Norman Rockwell after he moved to Arlington, Vermont, a town not far from Hoosick Falls. Like Grandma Moses, Rockwell created art that appealed to a broad audience.

On Display

Grandma Moses' paintings remain popular, and companies continue to use them on a variety of products. However, art galleries and museums are the only places for the public to see the actual works. While some museums have one or two of Grandma Moses' paintings, others hold a significant number of her works in their collections.

The Kallir family is still involved with the Galerie St. Etienne. Jane Kallir, Otto Kallir's granddaughter, is one of the gallery's directors.

Galerie St. Etienne

As the site of Grandma Moses' first solo exhibit, the Galerie St. Etienne maintains a special connection to the artist. Grandma Moses' work remains central to the gallery's collection, with several of her paintings in its holdings. The Galerie St. Etienne also continues to stage exhibitions of her work on a regular basis. Grandma Moses' art fits well with the gallery's mandate. Galerie St. Etienne is known for specializing in **Expressionism** and self-taught art.

Bennington Museum

The world's largest public collection of Grandma Moses' paintings can be found at the Bennington Museum in Vermont. The year-round Grandma Moses Gallery features a rotating selection of her works. The paintings are organized by theme, allowing visitors to learn more about the artist's approach to specific subjects. Besides showing works from its own collection, the museum also brings in Grandma Moses paintings on loan from different museums and art galleries. It searches for other Grandma Moses' paintings to add to its collection as well.

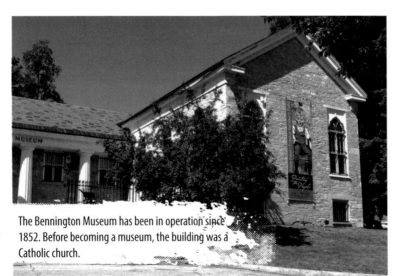

The Bennington Museum has been in operation since 1852. Before becoming a museum, the building was a Catholic church.

The Bennington Museum's collection also includes **artifacts** from Grandma Moses' life. Visitors can see samples of her embroidery, art supplies, and an 18th-century tilt-top table that Grandma Moses sometimes used as an easel. People can also visit the little schoolhouse that Anna Mary and her siblings attended from time to time in Eagle Bridge, New York. Moved to the museum in 1972, the schoolhouse is now an interactive center that explores Grandma Moses' life and the themes used in her paintings.

Metropolitan Museum of Art

New York's Metropolitan Museum of Art is one of the world's best-known art museums. It holds artworks from ancient civilizations all the way to present times, and includes an extensive collection of works by American artists. The museum has one Grandma Moses painting in its collection, along with six greeting card reproductions of her works. Her painting, *Thanksgiving Turkey*, hangs amid the display of Late Colonial Furniture in the American Wing, located on the museum's third floor.

The Metropolitan Museum of Art has more than 2 million works in its collection. It stages approximately 30 special exhibitions each year.

Write a Biography

All of the parts of a biography work together to tell the story of a person's life. Find out how these elements come together by writing a biography. Begin by choosing a person whose story fascinates you. You will have to research the person's life by using library books and reliable websites. You can also email the person or write him or her a letter. The person might agree to answer your questions directly.

Use the chart below to guide you in writing the biography. Answer each of the questions listed using the information you have gathered. Each heading in the chart will form an important part of the person's story.

Parts of a Biography

Early Life
Where and when was the person born?
What is known about the person's family and friends?
Did the person grow up in unusual circumstances?

Growing Up
Who had the most influence on the person?
Did he or she receive assistance from others?
Did the person have a positive attitude?

Developing Skills
What was the person's education?
What was the person's first job or work experience?
What obstacles did the person overcome?

Early Achievements
What was the person's most important early success?
What processes does this person use in his or her work?
Which of the person's traits were most helpful in his or her work?

Leaving a Legacy
Has the person received awards or recognition for accomplishments?
What is the person's life's work?
How have the person's accomplishments served others?

Test Yourself

1

During her lifetime, how many paintings did Grandma Moses create?

She painted almost 1,600 works.

2

How much did Anna Mary receive for the sale of her first paintings?

Her first paintings sold for $3 to $5.

3

Where was Anna Mary born?

Anna Mary was born in Greenwich, New York.

4

Why did Grandma Moses take up painting in her late seventies?

She took up painting because arthritis made it difficult to do embroidery.

5

Where and when did Grandma Moses have her first solo exhibition?

Her first solo exhibition was held in 1940 at the Galerie St. Etienne, in New York.

6

How old was Anna Mary when she married Thomas Salmon Moses?

She was 27 years old when she married Thomas Salmon Moses.

7

Who edited a book called *Grandma Moses, American Primitive*?

Otto Kallir, owner of the Galerie St. Etienne, edited the book.

8

What magazine featured Grandma Moses on its cover in 1953?

Time Magazine featured Grandma Moses on a cover in 1953.

9

Which painter put Grandma Moses in one of his paintings?

Norman Rockwell put her in a painting that was placed on the cover of The Saturday Evening Post.

10

What Grandma Moses painting was honored on a postage stamp?

The painting July Fourth was honored on a postage stamp.

Artistic Terms

The study and practice of art comes with its own language. Understanding some common art terms will allow you to discuss your ideas about art.

abstract: based on ideas rather than reality

brushwork: the way an artist applies paint with a brush

canvas: cotton or linen cloth used as a surface for painting

ceramics: articles made from clay that has been hardened by heat

composition: the arrangement of the individual elements within a work of art so that they make a unified whole

easel: a folding stand used to hold up a painting while the artist is working

engraving: a print made from an image cut into a surface

etching: prints made from images drawn with acid-resistant material on a metal plate

form: the shape or structure of an object

gallery: a place where paintings and other works of art are exhibited and sometimes sold

medium: the materials used to create a work of art

mood: the state of mind or emotion a painting evokes

movement: a stylistic trend followed by a group of artists

permanent collection: a collection of art owned by a museum or gallery

perspective: a technique used by artists to show space

pigment: fine powder that produces color; when mixed with oil or water, it becomes paint.

primary color: any of a group of colors from which all other colors can be obtained by mixing

proportion: the appropriate relation of parts to each other or to the whole artwork

space: the feeling of depth in a work of art

studio: a space, room, or building in which an artist works

Key Words

artifacts: objects made by human beings

commissioned: hired and paid for the creation of a piece of art

dimension: one of the elements or factors making up a complete entity

doctoral degrees: the highest academic titles given by a college or university

exhibit: to put art on public display

Expressionism: a style of art that emphasizes feelings and impressions over realism

fireboard: a piece of wood placed in front of a fireplace during the summer months

folk art: art created by the people of a region

landscapes: scenes or views of land, such as mountains, fields, and forests

luxuries: things that are nice to have but are not necessary for survival

palette: the range of colors used by an artist in making a work of art

panoramic: having a wide or complete view of a scene

prints: photographed or engraved images transferred to paper or a similar surface

prolific: to produce many things

rural: of the country, not a city or suburb

sugaring: the process of making maple sugar

tempered: hardened

tenants: people who rent or work land that belongs to someone else

tones: tints or shades of a color

Index

Log on to www.av2books.com

AV² by Weigl brings you media enhanced books that support active learning. Go to www.av2books.com, and enter the special code found on page 2 of this book. You will gain access to enriched and enhanced content that supplements and complements this book. Content includes video, audio, weblinks, quizzes, a slide show, and activities.

AV² Online Navigation

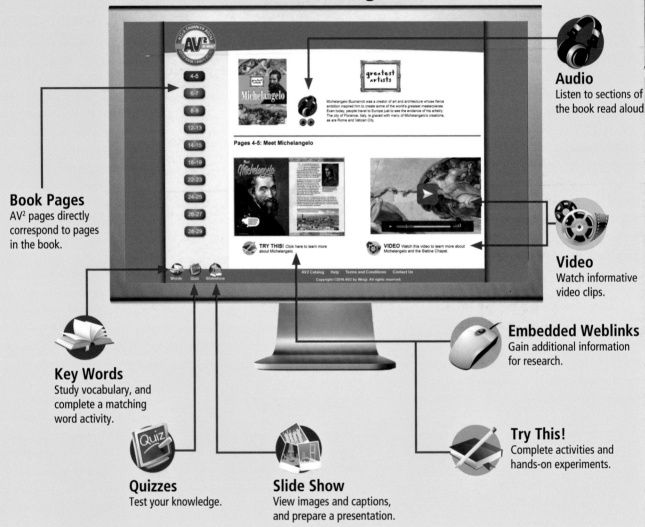

Audio
Listen to sections of the book read aloud

Book Pages
AV² pages directly correspond to pages in the book.

Video
Watch informative video clips.

Key Words
Study vocabulary, and complete a matching word activity.

Embedded Weblinks
Gain additional information for research.

Quizzes
Test your knowledge.

Slide Show
View images and captions, and prepare a presentation.

Try This!
Complete activities and hands-on experiments.

AV² was built to bridge the gap between print and digital. We encourage you to tell us what you like and what you want to see in the future.

Sign up to be an AV² Ambassador at www.av2books.com/ambassador.

Due to the dynamic nature of the Internet, some of the URLs and activities provided as part of AV² by Weigl may have changed or ceased to exist. AV² by Weigl accepts no responsibility for any such changes. All media enhanced books are regularly monitored to update addresses and sites in a timely manner. Contact AV² by Weigl at 1-866-649-3445 or av2books@weigl.com with any questions, comments, or feedback.